MICHAEL PHELPS

by Joyce Markovics

Consultant: Ellen Labrecque
Former Editor and Writer
Sports Illustrated Kids

New York, New York

Credits

Cover, © Mitch Gunn/Shutterstock; 4, © Matt Healey/UPI/Newscom; 5, © Richard Ellis/UPI/Newscom; 6, © Paul Kitagaki Jr./ZUMA Press/Splash News/Newscom; 7, © Daniel A. Anderson/ZUMA Press/Newscom; 8, Courtesy North Baltimore Aquatics Club; 8–9, © Jason DeCrow/Invision for SUBWAY/AP Images; 10, © Jerry Jackson/Baltimore Sun, Permission Granted by The Baltimore Sun Media Group; 11, © AP Photo/Anja Niedringhaus; 12–13, © PCN Photography/Alamy Stock Photo; 14, © Kyle Terada/USA Today Sports; 15, © Chris Keane/Icon SMI 329/Newscom; 16, © Patrick Schneider/KRT/Newscom; 16–17, © Nietfeld Kay A3390 Deutsch Presse Agentur/Newscom; 18, © Mark Reis/MCT/Newscom; 19, © Erich Schlegel/MCT/Newscom; 21, © Paul Kitagaki Jr./ZUMA Press/Newscom; 22TL, © Agencia Brasil Fotographias; 22TR, © Zakhar Chumak/Dreamstime; 22B, © kubais/Shutterstock; 23T, Courtesy North Baltimore Aquatic Club; 23B, © Chris Keane/Icon SMI 329/Newscom.

Publisher: Kenn Goin
Senior Editor: Joyce Tavolacci
Creative Director: Spencer Brinker
Production and Photo Research: Shoreline Publishing Group LLC

Library of Congress Cataloging-in-Publication Data

Names: Markovics, Joyce L., author.
Title: Michael Phelps / by Joyce Markovics.
Description: New York, New York : Bearport Publishing, 2018. | Series:
   Bearport's Library of Amazing Americans | Includes bibliographical
   references and index. | Audience: Age 5–8.
Identifiers: LCCN 2017010893 (print) | LCCN 2017012282 (ebook) | ISBN
   9781684022939 (ebook) | ISBN 9781684022397 (library : alk. paper)
Subjects: LCSH: Phelps, Michael, 1985– —Juvenile literature. |
   Swimmers—United States—Biography—Juvenile literature. | Olympic
   athletes—United States—Biography—Juvenile literature.
Classification: LCC GV838.P54 (ebook) | LCC GV838.P54 M37 2018 (print) | DDC
   797.2/1092 [B] —dc23
LC record available at https://lccn.loc.gov/2017010893

For more information, write to Bearport Publishing Company, Inc., 45 West 21st Street, Suite 3B, New York, New York 10010. Printed in the United States of America.

10 9 8 7 6 5 4 3 2 1

CONTENTS

The 2016 Olympics

Ready, set, go! It was a swimming **relay** during the 2016 Olympics. Michael Phelps dove into the pool. He sliced through the water like a bullet.

Michael leaps into the pool.

Michael takes a huge gulp of air as he gets ready to lift his arms out of the water.

The 2016 Olympics took place in Rio de Janeiro, Brazil.

Superfast Swimmer

Michael kicked extra hard. He bolted past the other swimmers and touched the wall. His teammate Nathan Adrian sped through the last lap. The U.S. team had won! The crowd went wild. Michael had won his 23rd gold medal!

Michael has won more gold medals than any other Olympic athlete.

After the relay, Michael celebrates with a teammate.

Michael holds seven world **records** in swimming.

Early Life

Michael Fred Phelps was born on June 30, 1985. He's the youngest of three children. Michael and his sisters grew up in Baltimore, Maryland.

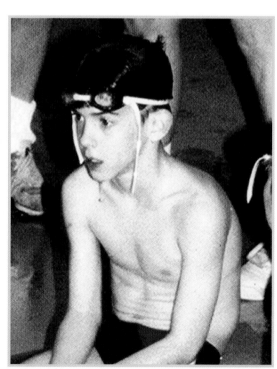

Michael as a boy at the North Baltimore Aquatic Club

Michael and his sisters,
Whitney (left) and Hilary (right)

Michael's sisters also enjoy swimming.

A Rising Star

As a child, Michael had a lot of energy. "He never sat still," said his mother, Debbie. She hoped swimming would **channel** his wild energy. So she took him to a nearby pool.

Michael's mom was right. Not long after he began swimming, Michael became calmer. And he started winning races!

Michael at age 13

Michael's mom at one of her son's races

As a boy, Michael was **diagnosed** with ADHD. This stands for "attention deficit hyperactivity disorder."

11

Record Breaker

By age 10, Michael was breaking youth swimming records. He was especially good at a **stroke** called the butterfly.

Young Michael continued to get better and better. At age 15, he was good enough to go to the 2000 Olympics!

Michael did not win a medal at the 2000 Olympics in Sydney, Australia. However, he did make the finals.

To swim the butterfly, Michael lifts both arms out of the water and swings them forward.

Built for Swimming

Why is Michael such a great swimmer? He's 6 feet 4 inches tall (1.9 m). He also has long, strong arms and huge feet.

Plus, Michael **practices**—a lot. To make it to the Olympics, he trained almost every day for six years!

Michael's long arms help him swim the backstroke.

Michael practices kicking his legs while using a paddleboard.

Usually, a person's arm span is the same as his or her height. Michael's arm span is 3 inches (7.6 cm) greater than his height!

The 2004 Olympics

In 2004, Michael swam in his second Olympics in Athens, Greece. He was just 19 years old. There, he won his first gold medal!

Michael stunned the crowd with his speed. In all, he won six gold medals and two bronze medals!

Michael warms up for one of his big races.

Because he's so fast, one of Michael's nicknames is the Baltimore Bullet.

Michael receiving one of his gold medals at the Athens Olympics

17

Eight Gold Medals!

At the 2008 Olympics in Beijing, China, Michael swam incredibly well.

In fact, he made history by winning eight gold medals. That's more than any other athlete had won in an Olympic Games!

Michael shouts for joy after winning another race.

Michael won eight golds in only seven days in Beijing!

After winning eight gold medals, Michael said, "Records are always made to be broken, no matter what."

19

Dreaming Big

Michael went on to compete in the 2012 and 2016 Olympics. He blasted away his competition.

In all, Michael has won 28 medals. This makes him the greatest Olympian of all time. "I was a little kid with a dream," Michael said. "If you dream as big as you can dream, anything is possible!"

After the 2016 Olympics, Michael retired from swimming. He was just 31 years old.

Michael greets his wife, Nicole, and his son, Boomer, after winning gold in Rio.

Timeline

Here are some key dates in Michael Phelps's life.

1980   1990   2000   2010   2020

June 30, 1985
Michael Fred
Phelps is born in
Baltimore, Maryland.

2000
Competes in the
Sydney Olympics

2001
Becomes youngest
male swimmer to
set a world record

2004
Wins six gold and two
bronze medals at the
Athens Olympics

2008
Wins eight gold
medals at the
Beijing Olympics

2012
Wins four gold and
two silver medals at
the London Olympics

2016
Wins five gold medals
and one silver in Rio
to become greatest
Olympian of all time

Glossary

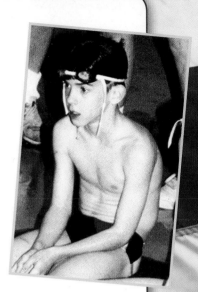

channel (CHAN-uhl) to direct

diagnosed (dye-uhg-NOHSSD) identified as having a medical problem

practices (PRAK-tiss-iz) repeats something in order to improve a skill

records (REK-urds) the best performances by an athlete

relay (REE-lay) a swimming race in which four teammates take turns swimming laps

stroke (STROHK) a swimming style

Index

Read More

Fishman, Jon M. *Michael Phelps
(Sports All-Stars).* Minneapolis, MN:
Lerner (2017).

**Phelps, Michael, and Alan
Abrahamson.** *How to Train with a
T. Rex and Win Eight Gold Medals.*
New York: Simon & Schuster (2009).

Learn More Online

To learn more about Michael Phelps, visit
www.bearportpublishing.com/AmazingAmericans

About the Author

Joyce Markovics has written dozens of books for children. She lives with her husband in a very old house along the majestic Hudson River.